Imperfect Mirrors
Indelible Myths

Bill Carpenter

IMPERFECT MIRRORS
INDELIBLE MYTHS

CONTENTS

Indigenous North Americans........1

First Music 3

Art into Writing.......................... 4

Pangaea Forever 6

Yosemite Valley............................8

Daphne and Apollo 10

Seasonal Nights 12

Winter Spirits 14

Solar Myths 15

Turtle Island.............................. 17

Niche... 19

Scales into Feathers.................... 21

River Mist................................... 22

The Centaurs.............................. 23

Goddess...................................... 25

Love Triangle.............................. 26

Creation Myth: Sea Star 28

The Water Loves the Land.......... 29

Creation Myth: Whales 30

Wind Dance................................. 32

Second Acts 33

Turtle Island II 34

The Kingdom of the Trees 35

Icebergs 37

Tridacnids 39

Ferns 40

Seasonal Birds 41

Autumn Alchemy 45

Spring Invasion.......................... 46

Dominical Beach Designs 47

Tidal Arts 49

Dawn, Hog Island, Maine 50

Hooded Mergansers 51

A Congregation of Turkeys......... 52

Of Birds and Skies 54

Jonah... 55

Ghosts and Where to Find Them . 57

Symbolic Speech......................... 59

Sculpting with Clay.................... 61

Symbols....................................... 62

Haiku Sextet............................... 63

In Verse* 64

In Emily's Garden 65

Sawing... 66

The Persistence of Song 68

Solids, Liquids and Gases........... 70

Clouds and Archetypes 72

Cuckoo Clock 74

Famous.. 76

Love Lies Bleeding* 78

An Encyclopedia of Knowledge.... 79

Either/Or 81

Imperfect Mirrors 83

Mirroring Avignon...................... 84

Light Speed 85

Carousel 87

Time Measure............................. 88

Eclipse of the Moon 90

Perspectives on the Moon 91

Mythic Journey 92

Multiverse 94

The Alchemy of Stars................. 95

Cosmic Enigma...........................96

Acknowledgements 97

About the Author............................98

Indigenous North Americans...

framed yurts
from the bones of mastodons
the ribs of whales
bound with sinew
and covered in animal furs.

Nights rich
with the scent of caribou
and whale oil
lit in soapstone lamps,
its hot liquid
bouncing light off
the low-slung ceiling.

These people who called themselves
after the animals they hunted:
the People of the Salmon and Caribou;
the Northern People of the White Bear;
the Ocean-Going People of the Cod;
the Ice-Bound People of the Seal.

They spoke of generations
before Europeans came in fishing ships
that could carry the sea's bounty
in hulls surpassing in bulk
the bellies of whales.

Beyond the horizon
they imagined
a future shrouded in fog,
on a low-lying island
only seabirds and seal inhabited,
where fishing was plentiful
and eggs freely gathered.

What more could a people ask of heaven?

First Music

Long ago
Paleo-humans
listened to birds
they mimicked
by whistling
or singing a cappella.
Until one found a
fan of feathers
he dried, plucked,

and scraped with flint
before breaking off
a length of wing bone
and unpacked mud
from his hollow prize
with a length of twig.

Believing this thin cylinder
held the secret of birdsong,
he attached feathers for their magic,
then putting pipe to lips,
blew sharply and repeatedly
till he heard a faint trill

the   *tur-reep tur-reep*
         tit-sui tit-sui

of the song
he'd been longing to sing.

Art into Writing

On cave walls, pictures
lost details and became words:
a flattened ⌣ stood for a bird;
an Î with a small circle over it was man;
a woman was an oval 0 to make room
for the magic she held.

The sun was a circle with radiating lines ☼;
the moon held its shadow ☽ close.
Lightning a crooked line ↘;
water two rippling lines ≋;
a circle with horns, an auroch ♉.
Shepherds kept track of flocks
by the number of such symbols
and counting was invented.

Fire was marked as a circle with peaks 🔥
which also meant spirit,
and when placed over someone's head
became a crown of gold for kings or queens
made from the fallen embers of the sun.

From marks made with sticks
tipped with charcoal, seasons were shown
by the sun's arc over land:
a high, bright sun was summer;
a lower, dimmer sun, winter.
Amulets of these symbols
were hung as necklaces and worn as jewelry.

The annual cycles of the moon
were named and counted,
seasons anticipated
in the first calendars.

From Lascaux, Chauvet, to Altamira
art evolved into language
marked on animal hides,
all decayed or lost.

People without art vanished.

Pangaea Forever

What if Pangaea never broke up,
there was no continental drift,
all the world still sutured together
like bony plates clustered
around the earth's skull?

South America still
conjoined to its African twin,
poking an elbow
into the dark continent's ribs.

No need for land bridges:
Russia and North America
forged together,
the bear embracing the eagle
in tectonic perpetuity.

Britain landlocked.
India displaced to
the southern hemisphere
with Australia and Antarctica.
All competing like hungry cells
merging with each other,
in an oceanic Petri dish.

All wars fought with armies,
no need for navies
or even shipping
in a world accessible
from Moscow to Sydney
by road or rail.

Boundaries blurred, so Alexander
might have extended his empire
to Costa Rica and Caesar
settled the American Midwest
as far as New Rome.

No Columbus, no Himalayas,
no Panama Canal, no Caribbean,
no Atlantic coastline,
the Gulf of Mexico a Great Lake,
Japan just another peninsula
stretching into the Tethysian Sea.
Much *less* diversity:
no kangaroo, koala or kiwi.
Madagascar cradled
between continents
like an overprotected infant.
Greenland stillborn
in the frozen limbo
of North America's womb.

And we all Pangaeans,
treading water
in the Panthallasic Ocean,
one massive ship
that never left its shores.

Yosemite Valley

From Glacier Point
the valley opens up
like the earth's stony labia;
sunlight glistens off
two-thousand-foot falls
spraying rocks
dark with moisture.

While shadows
obscure north-facing walls,
Half Dome rises
from the Y-shaped
Merced River valley.

A Red-tailed Hawk circles
low over the damp meadow
where Mule Deer forage
and parachute spiders
fill the air
with silky filaments.

A plaque says the valley
was formed by glaciers
over a million years,
eroding granite monoliths
while carving out the gorge.

But I can't help thinking
some moon must have crashed
into the Sierra Nevadas
and split into
Half and North Domes.

Or perhaps the Miwok legend tells it best:
a belligerent couple angers the spirits
with their wickedness
and are separated forever,
turned into giant granite pillars,
the dark varnish on the rock face—
the old woman's tears of remorse.

Daphne and Apollo

What madness
has Cupid wrought?

The eternal quest:
predator prey;
would-be lover
for his reluctant
maiden of the woods...

...and as Apollo reaches
for Daphne's ankle,
the springboard of her escape,
a vine encircles her calf,
creeps higher, entangling
knee and thigh,
its tendrils shred
her diaphanous robe,
tighten 'round succulent flesh
and pierce her maidenhead
as she gives herself to the forest.

She has stood her ground:
elongating toes taper downward,
dowsing the earth for nourishment
as she exchanges
skin for bark,
flesh for pulp,
blood for sap
out of fear, distaste or disdain
for her suitor's urgent passion.

And now it is Apollo
who is snared
in her branches of laurel,
her arborous embrace,

as he spins,
struggling to break free
from love's uncertain entanglements.

Seasonal Nights

From our back deck
tall pines and oaks
gerrymander night
into a puzzle piece
of sky.

Where we watch
evenings drift by
emblazoned with
the seasons'
constellations.

In summer
Cygnus spreads
her connect-the-dot
wings across our galaxy
faded by ambient light.

Looking north
we see the Big Dipper
swallowed
within the ghostly frame
of Ursa Major.

As fall settles,
Cygnus flies south
and Orion gathers his bow
to stalk the Zodiac
in search of Lepus
and other game.

While the twins waltz
across winter skies
inside their
house of stars.

With spring, Leo
ascends his throne,
Hercules in distant pursuit
reenacting his famous labor
strangling the beast
and hurling its hide
into the heavens.

With earth's greening, Cygnus
returns to her perpetual summer,
as a flock of geese honk
across the dark river of night
giving voice
to the swan's silence.

Winter Spirits

After the rain
snow and ice dissolve
into will-o'-the-wisps,
cold spirits freed
from the landscape.

The stick-figure forest
gives off a pale aurora,
softening focus,
rendering the material
ethereal.

A snowscape reshaped
by a sculpting wind,
exhaling clouds
as the frozen earth
breathes again.

Offering its moisture
as snowbanks dissipate
exuding waves
of trailing mist
from an icy sea.

As if a stage,
set with dry ice for fog,
where Hamlet roams
and the earth
gives up its ghosts.

Solar Myths

The ancients revered
the season maker
with calendars,
temples and observatories.

Believing a dark dragon
swallowed the sun each evening,
only to spit him up
each dawn.

Others saw a blazing
chariot cross the sky
into the western underworld
and reemerging in the east.

While our empirical mythology
predicts the sun
will morph into
a planet-devouring Titan,

a red giant evaporating
Mercury and Venus,
boiling away Earth's
oceans and atmosphere

before collapsing
into a ghostly
white dwarf, earth-sized
and still shrinking

to an unimaginably dense
black dwarf,
a perfect ebony diamond,
around which the outer planets

will orbit as they have for eons,
gems adorning this beautiful
but dead stone
with no light left to give.

Turtle Island

Our ancestors roamed the seas in canoes
looking for a place to settle.
They came upon a great humped island
where they beached their canoes.
It turned out to be an enormous whale
that shrugged and threw them back into the sea.

They paddled on and came to a volcanic atoll
that morphed into a sea serpent,
fire erupting from its blowhole
sending them back to their boats in terror.

Desperate to find land, they rowed on
to a gently sloping green hill of an island
where they made camp.
Again, the land rumbled, they realized
they were on the back of a giant sea turtle.

"Who dares trespass on my shell?" it bellowed.
The people pleaded to let them stay
the night to regain strength for their quest.
The great turtle agreed,
but only if they caught him a meal of fish.
That evening, the people tossed
a portion of their catch to the waves
the turtle ate at its leisure.

The next morning the turtle spoke again,
"I am old," the creature said,
"and have grown tired of my struggles.
You are resourceful people with your nets and fishing gear.
I will let you stay and make my back your home
if you agree to bring me fish every day before sunset."

The people stayed
and the turtle's back grew
into a land with trees and lakes.
Each evening they brought a portion of their catch
and offered it to the sea in gratitude.
They called the place Turtle Island.

Niche

Beneath a conifer
I slice away a section
of cauliflower mushroom,
an egg-shaped fungus
of interwoven rooms
and convoluted corridors.

At home I begin chopping
it up for the frying pan.
Its interior seems a model
for some multi-dimensional manifold
where particles appear and disappear
in unmeasurable ways.

Along one pathway
a dark tail whips around
disappearing into a floral fold.
Breaking into this hidden dimension,
a tiny dragon lies curled along a crevice,
a shiny brown salamander
with two beige stripes running its length.

It's traveled in my mushroom basket,
burrowed inside this labyrinth,
missing the tip of its tail,
I've inadvertently sliced off.
"Come see," I call to my partner,
who insists I return it in its truncated home
to a damp corner of the garden,
where she hopes it will thrive.

In the morning I check but find
only a dry and shriveled egg
minus its uprooted hatchling.
One can't tread softly enough
on this planet,
where no niche goes unoccupied,
no place too small
to call home.

Scales into Feathers

We were speaking
of Quetzalcoatl,
the plumed serpent
of Mayan legend.
How the idea of it
presupposes
the medieval dragon myth
and Archaeopteryx,
the link between
reptile and bird,
when we saw
a three-foot-long black snake
stretched across our path.

After nudging the snake
to safety,
we continued our hike
to the pond by the falls,
where we found curled
on the grass
a large snakeskin,
its tail fluttering in the wind;
a three-foot-long
diamond-scaled sheath,
around which were scattered
the feathers of the white bird
it had apparently molted into.

River Mist

At dawn
the sleeping river
sheds its skin
in a sinuous mist
slithering over
embankments,
a ghostly serpent
rising above
its fluid body
to unhinge its jaw
and swallow
the landscape
before the sun rises
high enough
to evaporate
the insatiable
apparition.

The Centaurs

"Native Americans...... were terrified of their first encounter with horses—as the totally foreign Spanish Conquistador on horseback initially resembled a single ominous creature...."
THE NATIONAL MUSEUM OF THE AMERICAN INDIAN

Human torsos rise
from equine chests,
manhood grown from
a quadrupedal beast
its massive loins
and galloping hooves
incarnated from
an ancient mythology.

Conquistadors galloping
on clouds of dust,
sun glinting
off armored skin
wielding long knives, capable
of separating a man from his head.
Casting spears and arrows
like gods from on high.

An advancing sunrise,
the army of Helios,
in search of the sun's fallen nuggets,
gold in masks and jewelry,
glittering shards of light
adorning temples.

From island ships,
with tall, cross-branched trees
hung with animal skins,
came priests with tales of a God
demanding the return
of the Sun's ransom.

This warring Horseman
of the Native American apocalypse:
Pestilence, Famine & Death to follow.

Goddess

She wears a rainbow for a scarf
over a peignoir of woven stars

the night knits a luminous net
of moonlight through her hair.

From one ear Jupiter hangs
encircled by satellites,

below the other, Neptune spins
a brilliant star sapphire.

Her skin radiant with nebulae,
a blush of starlight on her cheeks.

Though she wears no veil
her face is shadowed in eclipse,

her figure draped
in a tapestry of constellations.

It is said her beauty caused
men to weep oceans of tears

so she might see her reflection
mirrored in those saline depths,

as in her womb, light congeals
and galaxies are born.

Love Triangle

The Land basks
in her suitors' attentions,
aroused by Sky's
torrid caresses,
lifting her tidal skirts
to Ocean's brine,
blushing in foreplay,
she gives herself freely to both.

But Sky is a jealous lover,
smothering Land,
turning green at
Ocean's advances.
Sky scrolls love letters
on clouds to dissuade Earth
from Ocean's pandering.
His missives range
from pastel dusks and dawns
to dark rants billowing wrath.

Nor will Ocean
willingly share the lover
he cannot stop kissing.
As they lie together
beneath suspicious heaven,
hopeful of touching
places only Sky can reach,
Ocean washes ever higher
up the rocky knees of her shores.

This struggle unravels
as heartache for Land's inhabitants,
who thrive on the planet's
marbled blue harmony,
but cower when Land
spurs her suitors to jealousy
as they whip up cyclones
and ocean-driven maelstroms,
when all earthlings can do
is pray to their gods,
amid the throes
of these tempestuous lovers.

Creation Myth: Sea Star

An ancient god plucked a starfish from the sea
and stretched it two-hundred-thousand-light-years wide
into an enormous spiral wheel, that s/he
set spinning with a flick of a finger, then set aside.
Its atoms became the grist for stars and dust,
held together with gravity's glue,
its spiral arms stirring a bubbling must
on a path of birth or destruction, no one knew.
Each arm working as a giant claw
a luminescent being, adrift in time and space,
sweeping everything into its ravenous maw
devouring realms, leaving nary a trace.
But along its path new worlds, too, were born
condensed from clouds of cosmic debris
which were rendered, ripped and torn,
forging the elements with its alchemy.

Toss back any sea star beyond high-tide's reach,
they are galaxies marooned on an earthly beach.

The Water Loves the Land

The water loves the land
washes her feet
along sandy beaches,
bathes her in rain,
soaks her in bays
and scrubs her
with rivers and streams.
Water quenches earth's thirst
with lakes and ponds,
moistens her skin
with dew and mist,
polishes her rough edges
in a caress of waves,
cleanses her
of dust and debris
and blocks the drying sun
with moist clouds.
The ocean
is the earth's lover,
seducing her
with its million tongues.

Creation Myth: Whales

I. Gray Whales

They rise
with a "humph"
and a misty exhalation
on Magdalena Bay,
backs encrusted
with barnacles and amphipods
surfacing as dark arcs of sky
trailing star clusters,
nebulae and comet tails.

Toting a seafaring galaxy,
along spines
ridged with knuckles,
they have come to mate
and calve in sheltered lagoons.
Surfacing and submerging,
lifting flukes
and plunging into the deep
leaving behind
massive oval footprints
in their wake.

II. Belugas

While in Arctic nights
belugas surface and dive
carrying daylight
along their flanks.
Ghosts from
the top of our world,
measuring time
like pale hands
ticking along
our spherical clock.

Do these leviathans
drive the cycles
that spin our planet?
Belugas rising like the sun,
bleeding luminescence
as they plunge into the deep,
while grays weave night
into tropical seas.

Who better to carry our myths,
having journeyed from oceans
to amphibious shores
and conquered the earth,
only to return to the sea
to thread our oceans
with cycles of light and darkness.

Wind Dance

Wind waltzes with trees
runs his fingers through
leaves and needles, combing
away beetles and caterpillars.

The forest trembles
as her canopy bows
in submission.

A gust dips a sapling
nearly horizontal;
relenting, the wind lifts
her back into his arms.

Wind always leads
whether a gentle samba,
lively fandango
or torrid Apache.

Most dare not refuse
his requests
though some old trees
resist the wind's advances.

Steadying for the day he
will wreak vengeance
leveling the weary and the weak
beneath his relentless gale.

Second Acts

Dusk draws its curtain
as night opens the first scene
of its long running
two-act play with day.

The moon takes center stage,
casting Poseidon's net of light,
trawling ocean tides
for Cancer and Pisces.

The stars take their places
within this Greek chorus
as the earth dreams
of other worlds.

Fireflies mimic the firmament,
dusty-winged moths
assume the night shift
from butterflies and honey bees.

Insects drone
as peepers bellow
bass blues songs from
darkened stages.

Night's sketch follows
day's finished canvas,
a tranquil finale
to the first act's brilliance.

Turtle Island II

Flying west over the Rockies,
mountain range after mountain range
as far as eyes can see,
rows of peaks, horny outcrops,
evoke the Native American myth,
the scutes on the tortoise's shell.
Carrying the continent on its back,
lumbering at tectonic speeds
dragging the plates that form
the carapace, feet and head:
tail tapering along the curve of Central America,
left foot and toenails clawing away at the Aleutians,
head burrowing into the frozen tundra of the Arctic,
lifting mountains
as it buries beneath the ice
into the torpor of winter.

The Kingdom of the Trees

"rising up/in the waste places....
the second coming of the trees."
WENDELL BERRY

Our back yard overlooks
a kingdom of trees:
deciduous, fir and pine
living in apparent harmony,
ready to spread their
church of a thousand steeples.

Oaks tile the forest with mulch
and a harvest of acorns;
while pines drop
wooden flowers
packed with seeds
for birds and squirrels.

Some gather in ghettoes
of like-attired brethren:
fortresses of fir, shadowy
neighborhoods of hemlock,
pale-grey acres of thick-limbed beech
sheltering nurseries for their young.

Occasional spires of shagbark hickory,
yards of white picket-fence birch;
majestic old-growth oaks
throwing about massive arms
like preachers at the pulpit.

A realm littered with skeletons,
some leaning against
more youthful congregants,
others toppled,
lifting amphitheaters of roots.

All practicing the same
pagan faith of photosynthesis:
the energy of the sun
manifest in a leafy canopy,
held high on uplifted limbs,
in what passes for prayer.

Icebergs

From Cape Spear, Newfoundland,
North America sees its first sunrise,
wind and light carve their signatures
in an endless script of salt and foam.

While along Iceberg Alley
Arctic and Labrador currents
ferry a flotilla of ghostly ships;

their cargo the compacted
precipitation of eons, crystallized
water predating industrialization.

Each calved from glaciers
and carved by sun, wind and sea
into icy phantasmagorias:

winged sailing ships, tented spires,
spiked mountain ranges,
seafaring archipelagoes,

stabilized on their journey
by a vast unseen ballast.
They pulse with aquamarine flames,

as if the Northern Lights
lay frozen within,

layer upon layer of firn
absorbing ribbons of indigo

before melting into
this luminous armada

adrift on a cobalt sea.

Tridacnids

In shallow tropical shoals
orchids blossom beneath the waves,
where giant clams spill florid
mantles from half-open shells.

Not unlike the silk linings
of worsted suits,
layers of cream and sepia stripes
or iridescent folds of violet and blue.

Tridacnids, too timid to open
in the shadow of predators,
despite the death-trap myth
of deep-sea divers.

These satin flowers,
worthy of Georgia O'Keefe,
sense their world in shadow and light
along Pacific reefs.

All this beauty just to filter-feed
and soak in the sun's nutrients.
Scalloped boxes
stuffed with ornamental packing

as if to display
a pearl
hidden within
its lurid lips.

Ferns

Our lawn edged with ferns,
ostrich and cinnamon,
with roots to the Devonian
surviving the great extinctions
of the Permian and Cretaceous from
asteroids, hothouse gases and global ice ages.

A plant almost no animal eats,
grows unheeded beneath conifers
and leafy forests;
yet whose new growth,
spiraled into fiddleheads,
is a delicacy when sautéed in butter.

Each open frond recalling:
the fossilized skeletons of fish,
the feathers of dinosaurs and birds,
a dense array of photosynthesized
bones I struggle to keep
outside the yard's perimeter
with clippers and lawn mower.

This feather, this fan with spores
tattooed on its underside
in repeating lines from a poem
written in a code of dots.
This template displaying
the blueprints for the structure
of vertebrates, the membranes of flight,
an ancient flag of floral earth
prescient of what the future holds.

Seasonal Birds

I. Autumn

Feasting on acorns
for their southern trek,
Wood Ducks peel back
the curtain of daylight.

With their exodus,
green yields
to copper,
grasses turn golden

while trees shed
almond and bronze scales
burying summer's
faded carpet.

II. Winter

From Arctic climates
Snowy Owls unfurl
winter's white
over temperate latitudes.

Covering everything
with downy flakes,
while freezing lakes
with their icy breath;

whitening
the landscape,
as camouflage
from hapless prey.

III. Spring

With the thaw
phoebes and robins spread
lengthening days.
Worms free to tunnel,

loosen soil
from winter's grip
as clouds of insects
cloak the landscape,

awakening dawn
with birdsong.
Everything stirs and
is alive.

IV. Summer

Warblers of every stripe
weave yellow through fields
and forests, mirroring
dandelion and forsythia.

Bright as the rising sun
illuminating
bluebirds, goldfinches
and the oriole's tangerine.

Stretching light
to its limits
before night again wrestles day
back against the stars.

Autumn Alchemy

Autumn rich
with precious metals;
the bronze and copper
of oak and beech
carpet the earth
with fallen coins.

A golden landscape
of solar alchemy
gilding trees and grasses
with sunlight.
The gold we pan from streams,
mine from sunsets
buried in rock,

we hoard
to adorn our temples,
hammer into glistening discs
and hang in dark alcoves
to brighten winter nights.

The element we shape
into everything
synonymous with light,
from wedding rings
to the crowns of kings.

Spring Invasion

Edged with forest, our lawn
readies for the assault
as maple, cherry, poplar and oak
gather air and ground forces,
awaiting the winds of May,
when oak catkins pollinate the air
with mustard-colored dust,
discarding its spent garland
like dull Mardi Gras beads

As maples launch their air force
of single-winged copters,
parachuting in a twirling assault
covering every inch of lawn's measure.
Poplars explode in profusion,
their cotton spawn
falling like a warm spring snow
mimicking winter's mantle.

Tree roots tunnel into unclaimed territory,
oak, maple and sassafras saplings
catapult the perimeter
as bull briar and blackberry straddle the periphery.
The attack continues all summer
culminating with fall's bombardment
of acorns, pinecones and hickory nuts,
little mines squirrels bury to aid the trees' insurgency.

Held back for the moment by the buzz of mower
fighting nature's advance, its rotary blade slicing the heads
off saplings and dandelions as it tosses more pollen
into the thickening cloud.

Dominical Beach Designs

At low tide
the beach is strewn
with swaying blossoms
shaped from tiny balls of sand.

Their petals waft
from central burrows,
meandering lines forming
sepia-toned flowers.

A tiny shell pops
from one tunnel,
ducks quickly back
at the sight of my shadow.

Eventually, a Lilliputian crab
scurries across the sand
with unexpected speed
rolling orbs of mud

in an apparently random display,
a labor suggestive of Sisyphus,
a life condemned to pushing endless
spheres of sand along the beach.

Is this a labor of excavation?
Has the tide cast this buckshot,
in its ebb and flow
into a sandy floral garden?
Or is some other
explanation the cause?

Later, I learn
these crabs are feeding,
extracting microorganisms from grit
while shaping pellets with mouth and claw,
discarding them serendipitously
in elegant bouquets
across the beach.

Tidal Arts

The tide paints the bay blue,
fills the harbor to the base of docks,
carves a crescent beach
where there was muddy basin,
strewn with rocks
draped brown in kelp.

The sea surges to obscure the land,
smoothing over stone and boulder.
Later, it withdraws,
unveils the landscape
it swallowed;
returns the coast's
jagged contours,
its drab tidal flats.

Every six hours
a restless hand
sketching and erasing,
erasing and sketching.

Dawn, Hog Island, Maine

Song erupts at first light—
the pennywhistle tweets of sparrows,
the barking of crows,
a loon's forlorn wail,
a Wood Thrush's lisping allegro,
the flapping of wings on the ocean's skin
as the cormorant strums its way to flight
to the siren call of herring gulls
as a robin sings reveille.

Even the eye imagines music,
islands pulse
in frequencies of fir and pine
reflected off bays
mimicking decibels on a graph,
each tree a pitch
played to the rhythm of waves.
While their granite bases
are gouged with sonogram-like markings,
ascending and descending trills
scratched in an avian tongue.......

before the noise of lobster boats
chugging to harvest.

Hooded Mergansers

Ever wary,
a raft of mergansers moves away
as I approach pond's edge
displaying their tailored beauty:
wavy white pinstripes
against a dark mantle,
like an ancient symbol for water;
formal dickey strung from their necks
alongside rich chestnut flanks;
and white hood trimmed in black,
a sail crowning these miniature ships.

Three males moving away
from my line of sight,
a convoy shielding a cluster
of grey-brown females,
their spiky crests emblazoned in sunlight.
A small armada, reminiscent
of the Nina, Pinta and Santa Maria,
their sails translucent in backlit dawn
like candlelit ships set adrift.

Just yesterday,
I watched another group
from inside a blind of reeds,
two males lifting from the water
to thrust and cock their heads in display,
driven by some ancient mechanism,
an invisible cam lifting and lowering,
pitching and rocking
like carousel animals
or dancers on a wet stage
rehearsing their annual ballet.

A Congregation of Turkeys

Late afternoon, they strut
single file across the lawn,
somber, dark coats
shouldering beaked, wattled faces
like Puritans in procession.

Three hens, each
with a half-dozen poults in tow,
heads bobbing
in a slow, cautious march,
ever wary of ambush.

Freezing regularly
as if any movement
would render them suddenly visible,
like some predator-prey version
of red light, green light.

They linger in shadows
scratching and pecking
along the edges
of the forest's leaf litter
or under the bird feeder for seed.

Eventually, the hens
beckon their chicks
with a series of clucks.
As the brood gathers,
their mothers lead them
to a copse of pine trees.

Flapping noisily,
one hen launches herself
at a forty-five-degree angle
into a witch's broom
of dried pine needles,
where she continues her calls.

Wishing to follow,
but new to flight,
the poults scramble up fallen trees,
inclined ramps into the canopy.
Others hop, with feet and feather,
making their way up
a succession of branches,
a Jacob's Ladder of ascension.

The chicks eventually muster
courage and thrust themselves
the shortened distance.
Some undershoot and drop
like fallen angels.

A half-hour later
all have made their way
to night's roost,
a safe haven of pine boughs
in the elevated darkness.

Of Birds and Skies

"The bluebird carries the sky on his back."
HENRY DAVID THOREAU

On overcast days,
is it the Gray Catbird
that totes the sky on his back,
wearing a black thunder cloud for a cap?
Perhaps it's the Northern Cardinal
weaves the horizon with red
at dawn and dusk.

If so, it must be the Snowy Owl
carrying winter's pale banner
across northern latitudes,
when I yearn for blue skies
dappled in downy clouds.

For now, I'll sit in the rain,
under my umbrella,
occasionally lowering it and looking
to see which great black bird
is pulling night's shade
across the heavens
as the sun sets in a swirl of orange
where an oriole is settling in the west.

Jonah

after August Wilson's *Gem of the Ocean*

We were bound together
in a chain of human misery,
flogged as we were driven to the shore
where the leviathan waited.
Paraded up a plank
into the dark rank of its belly,
shut away from land and sun,
chained together
with some bread and water
to carry us through our long gestation.

This sustenance wasted rather than sustained us,
as we huddled for warmth,
rising and falling, a tide within a tide
in the endless blackness, wallowing in the filth
of our excrement, vomit, sweat and blood.
Our flesh withering to skin-covered bone,
our spirits atrophied as death metastasized
through the limb-choked gullet of the beast.

Rising and crashing as the behemoth
plunged on, through who-knows-what
seas and storms, our skin abraded
with the constant thrust and tumble
embedding us with festering sores.
Surely, we would all die, slowly digested
in the acid bath of its bowels.

And then, with all hope of survival long abandoned,
our terror faded to numbness,
our minds steeped in shadows of the life we had known,
the beast spit those of us still breathing onto this unfamiliar
shore,
where pale, ghostly men, waited with whips
to take us to our labor in the fields of our new-found nightmare.

Much later, when I learned the stories of the Bible,
I took the name Jonah, to remind myself
and others of my story.
Though I search the Good Book and my life
to find God's purpose in my mythic journey–
I can find no deliverance.

Ghosts and Where to Find Them

It takes a lifetime
for a house to give up its ghosts,
though the dead rarely stray from old haunts.

Decades sitting in the same chair,
the cushion wears the contours
of an invisible presence.

My mother still hears my father
wandering the hallway at night
trying to find his way back to her bedside.

Even in death, he is stricken with dementia,
her memories caught in the gears
of his perseverations.

Water dripping evokes his nightly voids;
the rocking chair sways to his absent rhythms;
the mind, too, warps time and place.

Alive, he thought her his long-dead sister,
his bridge to the present eroding
under collapsing infrastructure.

Will my mother visit me in my dreams
after her bed
swallows her in its wake?

Do the dead also yearn for their loved ones?
We too will fade to ghostly moons
phasing in and out of the memories of the living;

the only afterlife we know,
their memories breathing life
into the next generation of ghosts.

Symbolic Speech

More and more
she resembles what
she will become:
cheeks hollow, skin sallow,
her hands a blue/grey knotting
of bone and vessel
stretching a thinning
bruised skin.

She'd lost twenty-seven pounds.
Today, unable to sip water from a straw
to moisten parched lips.
She examines her hands
as if not sure who they belong to;
they wander restlessly over her bed sheets
pulling at her oxygen tube,
tugging at the rings loosely encircling her fingers.

It's been nearly a year,
this rehearsal for her final resting place;
she's not left her bed in six months,
settling into the foam of mattress and white sheets
like a stone washed up on the beach.

I change the television channel
back to a light music station
from the soaps her nurse's aide favors.
I take her hand in mine
surprised by the warmth emanating
from such a seemingly cold appendage.

These small kindnesses
seem inadequate for this woman
who brought me into the world,
who nurtured me beyond
the need for nurturing.

Agitated, she tugs at her rings ineffectively.
I remove them, let the oxygen tube
fall by her side.

I look for meaning in her gestures,
what the hospice nurse calls "symbolic speech,"
as if death were an Ingmar Bergman movie rich in portent.
The meaning
is in the life lived
not her passing,
and this is a good woman,
whose later life was mostly trial:
my father's early Alzheimer's,
her several breakdowns,
the death of a pre-teenage granddaughter.

Whoever said,
"God never gives a burden you can't bear"
must have led a sheltered life.
In the end she grew silent,
withdrawing to an inner world
that seemed nonetheless turbulent.

Still, she brought love,
led her four boys to a better future,
sacrificing herself in an act of redemption
for that peace of mind
that eludes her
even in death.

Sculpting with Clay

The gods shaped man from earth,
sometimes adding liquid to the medium
from which he is made
and to which he returns.

Enlil mixed clay with blood,
while Ninmah added water from the underground,
the Earth Maker dried his creations in the sun,
while Jehovah gave life to Adam from dust.

My daughter at five, made mudpies,
sometimes adding arms, legs, a head.
I remember her bending close to one creation
as if to give it breath.

And wishing, at the time,
I could take up her play and fashion a golem
to protect her from any boogeyman
feasting on the fragility and innocence

of a child made from clay.

Symbols

When I cast my lure
into the lake
I reel in the word FISH.

Every advance
moves us away
from the thing itself.

Every abstraction lacks
the heft, the texture
of this world.

Right now, I've fallen
out of bed reaching
for an element in a dream.

Only the hardness
of the floor
wakes me from my reverie.

Will we wake from this life
into a dream of pure being
yearning for the things we once held?

Here, take this word FISH
feel it wriggling in your hands,

struggling to slip
back into the mist
rising off the lake.

Haiku Sextet

If we only spoke
in the language of Haiku,
what a thoughtfulness....

bees abuzz bending
clover stems close to the earth
as if pole vaulting....

hummingbirds making
silent music with trumpet
vine blossoms blaring....

peepers orchestrate
cacophonous symphonies
in washboard rhythms....

cicadas drone in
endless counterpoint
mimicking bullroarers....

as....

summer stretches
between equinoxes, the
sun sets back its clocks.

In Verse*

for Wendell Berry

The farmer-poet furrows rows of seed
across the margins of his landscape in
a growing font of loosely flagged stalks
of corn, an enjambed stanza of equidistant
lines. Turning his tractor like a pen stitching
what will be written across this level field,
or his pen like a tractor pulling a plow and
when the season is right and the corn/font
has flourished to its full height, the farmer-poet
will cut a ghostly metaphor through the center
of his crop, a corn maze within the stalks,
a phantom image that can only be seen from
the perspective of a reader or a crop duster
flying overhead, perhaps drawn in the shape
of a tractor sowing, or a pen spelling lines of
poetry across the perfectly ordered rows of maize.

* *Verse: Old English* fers, *from Latin* versus *'a turn of the plow, a furrow, a*
  line of writing', from vertere *'to turn'; reinforced in Middle English by Old*
  French vers, *from Latin* versus.

In Emily's Garden

Irises strut
take center stage
like Victorian ladies
at a grand ball,
donned in ruffled bell sleeves
bustles and bustiers
of soft yellows and violets.
Backs straight
heads high
waltzing to the wind's
two-step.

Sawing

We saw felled limbs
and toppled trees
into manageable sections,
haul them to the garage
to cut into logs.
Oak and maple
poplar and cherry.

I load them thick or thin
onto a wooden trough,
overlapping its lip
a log length
and begin working the blade
back and forth.

The saw's steel teeth bite into bark
with their lettering
of narrow pointed Vs
and sharp-tongued inverted Ys
singing a song of severance
with its run-on sentence.

It's a rhythmic endeavor,
cutting wood
into cross-sectional lengths
for the fireplace.
Working the open handle
like a bow, sliding the blade's
lethal font across the grain.

When enough logs have fallen
we gather and carry them to the woodpile
to stack in bins, like wooden coins,
adding up to a number
with several hundred zeros,
a stockpile of savings
for wintry nights.

The Persistence of Song

Do you hear the melody
of our conversation
the common refrains
the way my breath rhythms
the soliloquy of your song
rising and falling in pitch and timbre.

The repeating themes
of self and other
melding our duet
the frequent asides to the cat
eliciting her silence
to our dialogue.

The sounds of each day:
morning's clink of ceramic mugs;
the whistling of water
at high boil; the recitation
of front-page headlines.
Summer evening's background
ballgame on the radio
the familiar voices announcing
the pitch count.

The way we're never aware
of the clock's ticking
unless alone at night
asking the other
"to come to bed"
and settle back into sleep
like the two boats at dock
we are, swaying
to the swells of our breathing,
the tides of our dreaming.

Solids, Liquids and Gases

Some ideas take you by storm in sleep,
only to deflate with daybreak.

Trivial upon reflection, they lose
the edge they held in restless hours.

Last night, I marveled all living things
are made from the three states of matter:

the dense fleshy substance of solids
suffering the dings of assault and abrasion;

their membranes enclosing rivers
of blood and bile, each cell's watery secretions;

the stomach with its acid baths,
the urethra flowing with streams of toxins;

as we inhale and exhale gases
inhabiting us like occupying spirits.

That these three material states
comprise all living things

(needing only a bioelectric
spark to ignite awareness)

might be stating the obvious,
and I, a fool for noting it.

Yet, the idea appeals to one's
sense of symmetry;

just one more of life's templates
building our world from what's at hand.

Clouds and Archetypes

I'm compiling an inventory
of cloud formations
(not the scientific variety)
but a survey of the shapes of clouds,
every wind-carved vapor pattern
drifting overhead on the sky's blue canvas.

Just yesterday, a wispy trail of moisture
held a ten-mile-long feather
complete with a centrally placed
quill radiating downy barbs
before tapering to a perfect oval tip.

It seemed as if the sky were sketching
one of earth's iconic archetypes
stippled in a pointillism of water particles.

Over the history of earth's evolution
can there be any doubt, at one time or another,
a pale Mona Lisa drifted overhead
in the swirling serendipity of our atmosphere?

Surely, a ghostly rebirth of Botticelli's Venus
once rode the magic carpet of evaporation
in a fair semblance of our modest maiden.

We've all seen a menagerie of earth's creatures
in the few hours spent musing over cloud formations,
as if they were generating
a Noah's ark bestiary, a will-o'-the-wisp
circus train of the animal kingdom.

All sketched in striations of moisture
randomly stitched together in an atlas
of the beings and places of our planet,

not unlike the gaseous nebulae of the cosmos
named for the shapes they mimic:

Horse Head, Crab, Cat's Eye, Hourglass,
Crescent, Owl, Boomerang, Coalsack-

those distant gardens of dust and minerals
where all being is birthed.

Cuckoo Clock

Each hour they spring
from a dark chamber of gears
to pirouette, waltz or cakewalk,
circling in raucous delight
like children
on Christmas morning.

They've been rehearsing all their days,
these oft-repeated routines
gone on too long to sustain our pleasure
while theirs goes undiminished,
never tiring of singing the hour
with gongs, whistles and tweets
as if we might forget
time's advance.

Perhaps,
they'd seem more credulous,
earn our respect,
if they aged
incrementally:
dark hairs turning grey,
wooden bodies gnarled in pain,
shiny complexions grown
furrowed with the grain of years.

But their sole purpose is celebration,
marking each hour with youthful abandon,
never fearing what follows each herald;
rejoicing one moment
for each passing hour
before returning
to sequestered darkness,
immobility and silence
anticipating their next
mercurial reincarnation.

Famous

after Naomi Shihab Nye

The moon is famous to poets and lovers,
the sun to everyone and everything.

Birds are famous for their flight of song
while the whale's song is mostly lost to the sea.

Waves are famous to the beach
that carries their impressions
in sand dunes and mudflats.

The infant is famous to its parents
for mastering what almost everyone does:
suckling, smiling, crawling, grasping
and a joyous enthusiasm for peek-a-boo.

The wedding band is famous to the ring finger,
long after it's gone, the finger still wears
its encircling scar like a wrinkle in time.

Your hands have the constant attention
of your eyes, to which they are famous.

We are all famous to the mirror that greets us
and carefully reflects each of our movements
like the most intimate dance partner.

Fall is famous for its leaves,
spring for flowers,
winter for ice and snow

and summer, summer is famous
for long, warm days and nights
and swimming naked
in the moonlight under the stars.

Love Lies Bleeding*

Mercury Rising, Hot Summer Lips
Love Lies Bleeding
Lofty Lady, Moonlight Eclipse

Dusty Rose, Sweet Lifeberry
Love Lies Bleeding
Sparks Will Fly, Cha-ching Cherry

Trailing Peach, Easy Peasy
Love Lies Bleeding
Heatwave Blend, Nice'N'Easy

Purple Love Grass, Nonstop Fire
Love Lies Bleeding
Flame Thrower, Pink Desire

Healing Hands, Cherry Punch
Love Lies Bleeding
Early Girl, Honeybunch

Candy Box, Peachy Keen
Love Lies Bleeding
Big Mama's Sweet Tangerine

* all names of flowers or vegetables from Burpee Seed Catalogue

An Encyclopedia of Knowledge

the tree knows time
is a ripple of concentric circles

rocks understand
hot and cold
the texture of rain
that water expands when it freezes

only the ocean files a discography of the songs of whales
the sky knows light alone brings color

while the earth is mother to all things

the diamond rejoices in its many facets
believes it is a fallen star embodying sparkle

flowers welcome the dances of pollinators
with a chalice of nectar

a pinecone's accounts are tallied by squirrels

a stone knows it cannot be skipped across the lake
no matter how flat it makes itself

birds compute flyways
in ways even they don't understand

a scarecrow knows it doesn't need a brain

the moon recognizes its light is borrowed

you know happiness comes from making yourself useful

while I only know
how to amuse myself writing poems

Either/Or

I. Scientists say the Moon
formed when a Mars-sized planet
hit Earth, spewing enough rock
into space to form our familiar satellite

or

Maybe the Moon budded from a volcano
on the surface of the Earth and blasted
into space to become its own little world.

II. Some say, a massive Black Hole at the center of our galaxy
is the force spinning our Milky Way

or

Maybe it's just a Big Drain, sucking everything down
like dishwater through a hole in the basin of our galaxy.

III. It's believed the dinosaurs became extinct
when an asteroid crashed into the Earth
causing rapid cooling and killing off most plant life

or

Maybe Noah thought the dinosaurs were just too big and clumsy
to let on his Ark, so they all drowned in the Great Flood
with the bulk of humanity.

IV. It's thought the cosmos is mostly made up of Dark Matter
that doesn't interact with light, but holds the universe together
with its gravity

or

Maybe it's like Dark Money, that doesn't interact with the IRS,
hidden away in distant accounts and laundered into capital that
fuels a worldwide Black Market.

V. The Big Bang Theory contends the universe began
when an incredibly dense ball, containing all matter, exploded
into the expanding universe of today

or

Maybe the universe began as a chemistry experiment gone bad,
when some petulant deity cranked up his Bunsen burner too
high
and the test tube boiled over into the Pandora's box of troubles
we know today.

or

Maybe all of these things
are something else entirely.

Imperfect Mirrors

"For now we see through a glass, darkly; but then face to face."
1 CORINTHIANS 13:12

The lake mirrors clouds
as if the sky were a blue liquid

the ocean splinters the moon's visage
along its surface into a cubist montage

every raindrop holds a hologram
of the leaf it comes to rest on

does the forest tire of seeing its reflection
smeared across the surface of the pond

do the constellations recognize themselves
along the watery axis of the earth's spin

light turns every translucent surface
into a dim mirror

city puddles scatter streetlights
into random red and green slashes

birds confront dimly colored rivals
hovering in bay windows

while you turn to take notice
of every storefront's glass shadow

noting the ghostly personage
hoovering within its imperfect mirror.

Mirroring Avignon

In the walled city of Avignon,
above the Palace of the Popes,
a hill and garden give view
to the Rhône and its countryside.
The town spreads out in a sea of rooftops
cresting like red-tiled waves.
We descend the spiral walkway
to the cooing of pigeons
roosting in elongated windows
weathered in a dark cross-hatching
where the plaza lies in cobbled sunshine.
I take a photograph of this medieval scene
while listening to an old gypsy
play his accordion for tips.

Back home, in an art class
overlooking Narragansett Bay,
a woman paints a backdrop in yellow,
imprinting the sun on her watercolor canvas.
Each week she plots details on a grid
of a cobblestone plaza
where a young woman dances
trailing a red scarf.
She sketches a sunken garden
set in a medieval city square
where daubs of color morph
into pigeons and an old gypsy
playing his accordion
in the golden plaza
of the Palace of the Popes.

Light Speed

I sight my telescope
on the bright object
nestled in a silhouette
of pine branches.

Hoping for Saturn,
I'm disappointed to find
familiar Jupiter
twirling her necklace of moons.

Changing focus
to a medium star
I suspect is the god of war
bleeding red
like a Doppler-shifted lantern.

Otherwise, only faint
clusters of stars, nebulae
and dense overlays
of unidentified
constellations.

While all around
my narrow focus, fireflies
flash encrypted signals
along the dark
perimeter of forest.

Some streak like
miniature asteroids,
others pulse like quasars
in a low-slung sky
sparkling in bioluminescence.

Everything wants to shine,
whether with desire
or in celebration.
These lesser lights-
their own galaxy
messaging from
a light-nanosecond away.

Carousel

It was the rotation
that thrilled me,
the way the carousel animals
cantered faster
the farther away
from center.

Riding a black steed
poised mid-jump
in orbit around a staging
painted with rolling hills,
where a steepled village lay
nestled between mountains.

Circling this life-sized
music box
scratching out
honky-tonk rhythms
along its spinning disc;

in orbit with a stampede
of fanciful beasts,
an unlikely zodiac
in the sky around
this slowly
churning earth
beneath my galloping stallion.

Time Measure

Sundials mounted on church façades
or set as statuary in gardens
follow the arc of shadow
the sun casts across
Roman-numeral grids.

While the hourglass trickles
grains of sand
through narrow bottlenecks,
building miniature dunes
in inverted measure.

In the age of the machine
metalworkers built elaborate
housings for gears and pendulums
giving time a voice
ticking to industry's flow.

With the watch, time is always with us
tucked away on a chain in a pocket
or encircling a wrist
as if time were an amulet
asking the hour's blessing.

In the nuclear age, atomic clocks
measure billionths of a second
in increments infinitely divisible
noting even the beats between
the strokes of a hummingbird's wings.

In our digital age
time has slipped off its clockwise
belt to travel in a linear display,
a suspended, uninterrupted now,
we take for an eternity of moments.

Eclipse of the Moon

The earth's shadow
casts a red glow
as the moon dons
a Martian mask.
Taurus and Gemini
emerge in waning light
slinging this fiery
red amulet
in their cat's cradle of stars.

Perspectives on the Moon

The full moon
imprints itself on my roof

shadows its reflection
on earth's imperfect mirrors.

I look for migrating birds
transiting its narrow arc of sky

but see only wisps of clouds
passing in a lacy veil.

Through a spotting scope
its features loom

into dark and bright seas
pocked with impact craters

sprouting distal rays
like pale, embossed suns.

Pulling away from the glare,
the magnifying lens

refracts a fuzzy hologram
looking for a place to settle

I bend to cradle
this tiny,

lantern moon
carefully in my hands.

Mythic Journey

After six decades
the Parker Solar Probe
is on its way,
like some Greek hero
fleet as Mercury
gathering strength from Venus
to snap-the-whip
into orbit around the Sun.
Sailing through the Sun's corona,
buffeting solar winds, nuclear heat,
fire spewing off Parker's satellite
as it rips through
plumes of plasma
looping out and back
like waves on the beaches of Hades.

To touch the very star
ordering our alignment of planets,
fire walking across the cosmic coals
of our neighborhood.
Is it like Icarus doomed
to fly too close,
melt the wax from its wings
and crash into the inferno?

Or like Daedalus
live to tell the tale,
hitch its horses
to Apollo's chariot,
ride the solar winds,
transit our star's circumference,
pass through arches of flame
and like Prometheus
return with secrets
stolen from the workshop of the Gods.

Multiverse

A universe
among innumerable others

like bubbles blown from a child's wand,
a clustered cosmos shaped in foam

or nesting Russian dolls
of expanding or diminishing size.

A wax comb of octagonal tunnels
packed together like corrugated cities,

or an ever-erupting volcano spewing
black clouds from the bottom of a cosmic sea.

All set in a hall of opposing mirrors
lit to infinite regression

within the arc of space/time
till just thinking about it

makes my head hurt, wondering just
how much smaller we can get?

The Alchemy of Stars

Stars wield their magic
growing denser and hotter
combining and recombining
protons and electrons
in the wizardry of its alchemy–
these hydrogen-fueled nuclear furnaces
fuse helium and generate
temperatures many times our sun
until the lightest element is consumed.
When they turn their attention
to fusing helium into carbon,
into oxygen into nitrogen,
making heavier and heavier elements
up to and including iron.
Where fusion ends
and gravity sinks its iron ball,
that rebounds as a supernova,
the philosopher's stone,
filling out the periodic table:
gold, silver, titanium, lead,
copper, uranium, nickel and zinc.

No wonder the ancients worshipped our sun
as Helios, Horus, Apollo, Ra, Sol and Sulis
the creators and sustainers
of this earth
this life.

Cosmic Enigma

At the center of galaxies
voracious Black Holes
ingest matter and energy.

One-eyed goliaths
devouring everything comes near
on their journeys through space/time;
the cosmos a web of these
cosmic shredding machines
stretching matter into strings of molecules;

Taking light,
the universe's Rosetta Stone,
hostage in its gravitational gears,

where time stops,
photons and leptons collapse
in the infinite density of its vaults.

All lost to inescapable darkness,
where the laws of physics sleep
and dream of alien worlds

and we, like ancient mariners
spin myths of monsters and mayhem
beyond even our imagining.

Acknowledgements

Thanks to the listed publications, contests and websites for their encouragement by publishing the following poems:

1. *Seasonal Nights:* an animated version of *Seasonal Nights* was selected for the international REELpoetry Film Festival 2021.
2. *Turtle Island*: Surrounded: Living with Islands, Write Wing Press, 2012.
3. *Creation Myth: Whales,* Origami Poems Project, 2011.
4. *Goddess* and *Love Triangle,* Origami Poems Project, 2015.
5. *Icebergs* and *Spring Invasion,* Crosswinds Poetry Journal, 2016.
6. *Tidal Arts,* Crosswinds Poetry Journal, 2017.
7. *Haiku Sextet,* Earth's Daughters, 2016.
8. *Ghosts and Where to Find Them,* second prize, Galway Kinnell Poetry Contest, 2017.

About the Author

Bill is a widely published poet and member of the Ocean State Poets, who strive to provide an environment for self-expression through poetry. For the past twelve years, he has been one of a trio of poets facilitating a poetry workshop at the Medium Security Building of the Adult Correctional Institution in Cranston, RI.

His poem "Peace" received honorable mention in the Barbara Mandigo Kelly Peace Poetry Contest and "Ghosts and Where to Find Them" won second prize in the 2017 Galway Kinnell Poetry Contest. He produced an animated version of "Seasonal Nights," which was selected for the international REELpoetry Film Festival out of Houston, TX.

He lives in Chepachet, RI with his partner, Emily. They believe retirement is an opportunity to reinvent themselves through education and the arts.

www.ingramcontent.com/pod-product-compliance
Lightning Source LLC
LaVergne TN
LVHW051604080426
835510LV00020B/3119